THE BEST OF BRITAIN HERITAGE SE...

Darlington
Birthplace of the Railwa...

CW00538418

CONTENTS

The interesting and varied architecture along High Row in Darlington

Discovery Publishing (UK) Limited wish to thank all those persons, organisations, official bodies and their officers, for their kind assistance in the production of this publication.

Photographs reproduced by kind permission of Discovery Photo Library Ltd. Photograph marked (CM) courtesy of The Cornmill Centre. Photograph marked (CT) courtesy of The Civic Theatre.

The author and publishers of this book do not accept any responsibility for the accuracy of the general information, tours and routes suggested for travellers by road or on foot and no guarantee is given that the routes and tours suggested are still available when this book is read. Readers should take all elementary precautions such as checking road and weather conditions before embarking on recommended routes and tours. Any persons using the information in this guide do so entirely at their own discretion.

Cover photographs: (Top) Darlington's famous Clock Tower landmark as seen from Tubwell Row; (Bottom Left) Clark's Yard in Darlington; (Bottom Right) St Andrew's Church at Haughton-le-Skerne.

WRITTEN BY VERA CHAPMAN. EDITED BY CAROLINE HILLERY.
SERIES EDITOR AND DESIGN MALCOLM PARKER. ARTWORK AND DESIGN ANDREW FALLON.
PUBLISHED BY DISCOVERY PUBLISHING (UK) LTD., 1 MARKET PLACE,
MIDDLETON-IN-TEESDALE, CO. DURHAM, DL12 0QG. TEL: (0833) 40638. PRINTED IN ENGLAND.
ISBN 0-86309-108-3. COPYRIGHT DISCOVERY PUBLISHING (UK) LTD.

Introduction to Darlington

DARLINGTON is a busy market town and shopping centre surrounded by beautiful countryside. Main road and rail links with London and Edinburgh, a regional airport only 6 miles (10 kms) away and a network of local roads make it for residents and tourists alike an excellent centre for the major attractions of **Durham, Northumberland** and **Yorkshire**.

The River Tees near High Coniscliffe

Voted by the Civic Trust as one of the six best towns in which to live and work, its town centre, based on one of the country's largest market places, is a **Conservation Area** in which Georgian, Victorian and Edwardian buildings mix with vernacular and modern in a harmonious blend on a human scale. The town escaped the comprehensive redevelopment and high-rise buildings so popular in the post-war era. Its leafy suburbs are a legacy of the villas and parklands of the town's Victorian prosperity and of the careful design of the housing estates which were later built around them.

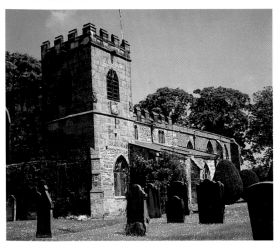

The magnificent St Peter's Church at Croft

Darlington has several claims to international fame. It was the birthplace in 1825 of the **Stockton and Darlington Railway** (S&DR), the world's first steam-hauled public railway, and went on to become a major railway engineering town. Nearby, at Croft, was the happy home where **Lewis Carroll**, author of '**Alice in Wonderland**', gained youthful inspiration and developed his writing skills. Darlington market was the centre for the pioneer breeders whose improved Shorthorn cattle were sent to stock the pastures of the New World.

Here, too, lived the first ever Quaker MP and the inventors of the first flax-spinning machinery. Darlington was also the birthplace of the first halfpenny morning newspaper, and is still a regional newspaper publishing centre.

THE BOROUGH OF DARLINGTON was founded in the C12th on an earlier Saxon settlement, when **Hugh Pudsey**, Bishop of Durham, built the Church of St Cuthbert, a Bishop's Palace and a Market Borough beside the River Skerne, with a separate manor of Bondgate for his bond tenants. His Early English Church and the medieval street pattern survive today, as do the ancient street names, Row, Gate and Wynd.

The pretty and peaceful village of Hurworth

Darlington became a Municipal Borough in 1867, and a County Borough in 1915. Stage by stage, the villages of **Cockerton, Haughton-le-Skerne** and **Blackwell** were absorbed. Finally, with the reorganisation of Local Government in 1974, Darlington became one of the eight Districts of the new County of Durham, taking in the villages and farmland of Darlington Rural District. Thus it became the new Borough of Darlington covering 20,000 hectares (49,000 acres) with a population of around 98,000.

The History of the Town

Prehistoric & Roman Times

EARLY SETTLEMENT in the area is evidenced by occasional finds: Neolithic flint flakes and arrowheads at Newton Ketton, a deer antler pick and an iron sword in a bronze scabbard at Barmpton and a Romano-British pottery lamp at Middleton St George. A supposed barrow at **Carlbury** near Piercebridge supports the evidence of cropmarks, revealed by air photography, of widespread settlement in the later prehistoric period in the lower Tees Valley where a number of sub-rectangular and D-shaped enclosures have recently been found.

Massive and complex earthworks at **Stanwick** are a major feature of national importance. Excavated by Sir Mortimer Wheeler shortly after the Second World War, they were then thought to be the late Iron Age defences of the Brigantes against the northward advance of the Romans. More recent investigations suggest a short-lived trading function, perhaps with the Roman south of England, at a strategic point where the east and west routes from Scotland converge.

Roman roads passed to the east and west of Darlington through Sadberge and Piercebridge. Where **Dere Street** crossed the River Tees at **Piercebridge** a late Roman fort, bridge and civil settlement have been excavated. Casual finds of Roman coins have been made at Cockerton, Haughton-le-Skerne and Ketton.

Saxon Darlington

Firm evidence of settlement at Darlington itself, however, does not appear until the Saxon period. The place-name itself is Saxon. Early forms include Dearthington (1050), Dearnington (1148) and Dirlington (1196). The derivation is uncertain, possibly 'the tun of Deornup's people'.

A pagan **Saxon cemetery** was found in 1876 on the Greenbank estate near Dodd Street. Six skeletons were accompanied by late C6th or early C7th grave goods. These included food vessels, bronze brooches, an amber necklace, iron shield bosses and iron spearheads, now in Darlington Museum and the Ashmolean Museum at Oxford.

IN THE CHRISTIAN ERA, tradition holds that the Saxon monks of Lindisfarne, wandering in flight after the Danish raid of 857 had sacked their monastery, rested at Darlington with the coffin of St Cuthbert before they settled at Chester-le-Street and in 995 at Durham.

In 1003, **Styr**, son of Ulphus, at a ceremony in York in the presence of King Ethelred and Archbishop Wulstan, gave Darlington to **Aldune**, the first Bishop of Durham. Darlington thereby became a manor of the Bishops of Durham, a situation which lasted until the C19th.

Between 1003 and 1016 a Saxon church was built on the bank of the River Skerne. Two Saxon crossheads, a Danish hog-backed tombstone and the foundations of an early church came to light in the 1860s during the restoration of the present **Church of St Cuthbert**. The crossheads and tombstone are now on display in the Church.

Traces of a rectangular ditch and rampart which supposedly defended or defined the Saxon settlement appear to be unverified. Recent archaeological excavations of its route behind Houndgate were inconclusive.

Unfortunately the Domesday survey of 1086 stops short at the River Tees, so we lack a descriptive and comparative account of places in Durham at that date.

The Medieval Borough

AFTER THE NORMAN CONQUEST and probably in the late C12th, Darlington was created a Borough, with burgesses or freemen and its own court presided over by a bailiff, a paid official appointed by the Bishop. The original charter is lost.

A separate manor of **Bondgate-in-Darlington** housed the Bishop's bond tenants or copyholders who, like the tenants of the adjoining manors of **Cockerton** and **Blackwell**, were administered by the **Bishop's Halmote Court**.

These manors, together with the Borough and the Archdeacon of Durham's manor of **Newton**, formed the ancient parish of

Darlington. Each manor had its own field system of arable land and common pasture, but some facilities such as mills were shared.

THE GREAT MARKET PLACE bounded by High Row (Headrow), Tubwell Row, Horsemarket and St Cuthbert's churchyard was probably laid out at about the time when Bishop Hugh Pudsey, nephew of King Stephen, built in 1164 his manor house or Bishop's Palace beside the Skerne and alongside it from 1180 onward, his new Early English Gothic **Church of St Cuthbert**. The manor house was in a small park, whilst across the Skerne, perhaps later, came the Bishop's High and Low Parks impaled by Bishop Bek.

Bishop Pudsey's survey of his manors in 1183, named the Boldon Buke, and Bishop Hatfield's survey of 1380 throw some light on Darlington Borough and manors.

The roads then called **Sadbergate, Swatergate, Bathelgate** (Coniscliffe Road), **Cockyrtongate** (Woodland Road), **Duresmegate** (Northgate), **Priestgate** and **Hurworthegate** are still today the main roads leading out of the town centre.

The Borough and Bondgate manor together had arable land in three fields, **Nessfield, Dodmerfield** and **West Field**, meadowland at **Ellingsmedowe** and **Polimpole**, and a common pasture recorded in later records at **Brankin Moor**.

Darlington Railway Centre and Museum

RENTS WERE PAID TO THE BISHOP in services and money. The villeins had to mow the Bishop's meadow, make and lead his hay, carry wood, wine, herrings and salt and lead carts on the Bishop's journeys. The pinder paid rent in corn, hens and eggs, whilst the dyers, bakehouses and mills paid in money. There was also a fishery. The Borough and Bondgate each had a forge. The cottagers of Cockerton drove cattle to the Bishop's Palace and cleaned it for his visits, whilst those of Darlington and Blackwell made haystacks, carried fruit and worked at the mill.

IN THE C14TH, wealthy Darlington wool merchants were exporting bales of wool to Flanders via the port of Newcastle, drawing supplies from as far afield as Cumbria, and helping to finance Edward III's expedition to France at the beginning of the Hundred Years' War.

Darlington was also engaged in the weaving, fulling and dyeing of **woollen cloth**, using the Bishop's fulling or walk mill and his dyehouse on the River Skerne until the end of the C14th. Bishop Hatfield's survey showed that by 1380 Darlington was by far the wealthiest of the Bishop's Boroughs of Gateshead, Sunderland and Durham.

Tudor Times - The C16th

Darlington's position on the **Great North Road**, the route between London and Edinburgh, brought visitors of national significance into the Borough in peace and in war.

In 1501 came **Margaret Tudor**, daughter of Henry VII, in royal procession on her way north to marry **James IV of Scotland**. She crossed at Neasham ford, and from Neasham Abbey was ceremonially escorted by a throng of mounted dignitaries to St Cuthbert's Church gate whence the dean and clergy of the district led her to the Bishop's Palace as his guest.

John Leland, appointed King's Antiquary by Henry VIII, approached Darlington in 1538 via Pounteys Bridge and Neasham. He noted a three-arched bridge over the Skerne, and thought Darlington the best market town in the bishopric except Durham. He remarked on the lively market of Darlington and the Bishop's pretty Palace. In St Cuthbert's Church he noted a long and fair altar stone in black and white variegated marble, and pointed out that the Church was collegiate, with a dean and prebends.

Between 1538 and 1544 the **Council of the North**, set up to control the border counties, sat at Darlington under threats of war with Scotland.

DURING THE REFORMATION and the **Dissolution of the Monasteries**, many northern families who supported the old faith aired their religious grievances in 1536 in an ill-fated protest march southward known as the **Pilgrimage of Grace**. To Henry VIII this was treasonous. In the retribution which followed, **Cuthbert Marshall**, Dean of Darlington, was a suspect and narrowly escaped implication.

The collegiate status of St Cuthbert's and the existence of chantry chapels therein brought it within the Act of 1547 for dissolving minor ecclesiastical foundations. St Cuthbert's lost its four prebends and its two chantries of St Mary the Virgin and of All Saints and became simply a parish church.

UNDER ELIZABETH I, Darlington was one of the chief centres of another unsuccessful revolt against religious persecution, the **Rising of the North** in 1569, led by the **Earls of Northumberland and Westmorland**. Darlington was to be the assembly point for the royal army, slow however to arrive. Meanwhile the Northern earls reached Darlington, made proclamation of loyalty to the Queen, but failing to take York, retreated and fled. Twenty-three Darlington, Cockerton and Blackwell men were hanged.

In 1585, as reported in a pamphlet 'Lamentable News from the Town of Darlington', a fierce fire swept the Borough. Two hundred and seventy three houses were burnt.

High Row and Skinnergate were gutted, and eight hundred people made homeless. Whilst these figures may have been exaggerated in a plea for relief, it was said that the flames could be seen from Roseberry Topping, a peak in the Cleveland Hills. The only buildings of the Tudor period to survive into the C19th were in the lower part of the town. The Nag's Head in Tubwell Row, originally the vicarage, was the last remaining Tudor building, demolished in the 1960s except for a rear wall retained in the rebuilt public house.

BY THE BEGINNING OF THE C16TH the woollen industry had declined, the fulling mill was dismantled and the dyehouse was out of use. Surviving wills for that century show that leatherworkers far outnumbered weavers, a situation confirmed by a list of pardons after the 1569 rebellion. Inventories show that tanners, who treated cattle skins with lime and oak bark solutions, were predominant. Tawers treated sheep skins with oil and alum. Leather searchers checked the quality of leather and of goods like saddles, shoes and gloves. The Glover family were tanners weavers and postmasters. By the end of the century,

however, the linen industry was of rising importance.

Stuart Times - The C17th

The surviving **Borough Books** for 1612 to 1633, elucidated by historian Norman Sunderland, confirm this situation and give a lively picture of the Borough. There were tanners, shoemakers, saddlers and glovers, and a cordwainers' guild. Leather was sold at Skin Hill in Market Place, and the fellmongers sold close by. Meat was offered at the shambles, while the fishmongers traded alongside; bread, oatmeal and food were near the tollbooth, and butter at the market cross. There were tinners and braziers, pewterers and silversmiths, potters and ropemakers, and sellers of cutlery and hardware. Live cattle and other farm animals were also on sale.

The market was ceremonially opened on fair days by the Borough bailiff in procession, and a bell rung for trading to begin. Hirings for farm workers were held on three days a year. There was a common bakehouse and a forge, and a ducking stool behind Northgate. Town wells in Skinnergate and Tubwell Row were supervised by overseers, and the stinted common pasture at Brankin Moor was still in use, regulated by grassmen.

TWO FURTHER ROYAL VISITS OCCURRED. In 1603, **James VI of Scotland**, journeying south to claim the English throne as James I, stayed at **Walworth Castle** at the hospitality of widow Jennison. In 1617, James revisited Darlington en route northward to Durham, staying at the cobble-built **Crown Inn** on the Prebend Row and Tubwell Row corner, where he made his oft-repeated remark, 'Darnton! I think it is Darnton i' t' Dirt'.

The Georgian Era - The C18th

THE BOROUGH BOOK of the period shows that in 1710 the Borough had one hundred and four freeholders. No doubt the Borough was slowly growing. Brankin Moor had been enclosed in 1674, and by the mid-C18th the Bishop had allowed buildings to encroach on to the market place at Bakehouse Hill. Later in the century a private survey in 1767 revealed a population of 3,295.

Darlington was still making **woollens**, organised as a cottage industry in which washed wool was processed in turn by wool combers, spinners and hand-loom weavers. By the mid-C18th, however, Darlington was more renowned for its **linens**. About five hundred looms made huckabacks, diapers and sheeting, tablecloths and napkins. Huckaback was a rough linen with upstanding threads suitable for towels. Diaper was a material with a small diamond pattern. Cloth up to three yards wide was marketed in London, Darlington being the only supplier of widths so broad.

Pease's House behind Horsemarket, Darlington

At first, handloom weaving was done in the surrounding villages like Cockerton, Hurworth, Neasham and Heighington. When **John Kendrew** and **Thomas Porthouse** patented the first flax-spinning machinery in 1787 they set up in a water-powered mill near St Cuthbert's, and later at Haughton-le-Skerne and Coatham Mundeville, before being ousted by Marshall's at Leeds.

The limy water of the Skerne was believed good for bleaching. It even attracted Scottish linen. There was a bleach ground and a bleach mill by the Skerne behind Northgate.

DURING THE REBELLION of **Bonnie Prince Charlie** in 1745, Darlington's situation on the Great North Road brought the English army under the **Duke of Cumberland** through the Borough. Warned that the soldiers were ill-clad for winter marching, the Darlington Quakers quickly made at their own expense vast numbers of flannel waistcoats ready for their arrival. Some of the soldiers camped in a field behind the Friends' Meeting House in Skinnergate. The Duke stayed with **James Allan** of **Blackwell Grange**. On return from the Battle of Culloden, he lodged at the **Talbot Hotel**, the posthouse on the corner of High Row and Post House Wynd.

The Duke denounced the road between Darlington and Croft as the worst he had ever travelled on. This was part of the Post Road, which became in 1745 the Durham to Darlington and Boroughbridge Turnpike Road, the first in County Durham. Other **turnpike trusts** empowered to improve road surfaces, erect gates and charge tolls were set up around Darlington: the Barnard Castle, Darlington and Stockton Road, in 1749; the Coal Road from West Auckland to Darlington in 1751; the Staindrop to Darlington Road in 1795; and the Angel Inn, Blackwell, to Barton Lane Ends Road with a new bridge over the Tees in 1832. Altogether there were twelve Turnpike Roads around Darlington, reflecting the growth of trade and industry in the early years of the Industrial Revolution.

AN AGRICULTURAL REVOLUTION was also going on in south Durham and north Yorkshire, centred on Darlington market. Farmers were improving the local breeds of Teeswater sheep and Shorthorn cattle. At first they bred for size and fatness. **Christopher Hill's Blackwell Ox**, slaughtered in 1779, weighed 162 stones, of which 11 were tallow. **Robert Colling of Barmpton**, 'the sheep man', went to study Robert Bakewell's methods at Dishley. He and his brother **Charles Colling of Ketton Hall** went on to produce sounder stock with good beef and milk potential by inbreeding carefully selected local Shorthorns.

The Ketton Ox, bred in 1796 and sold in Darlington market, travelled 3,000 miles (4,800 kms) as the Durham Ox, a showpiece until, dislocating its hip in 1807, it was slaughtered at 189 stones. **Comet**, sold by Charles on retirement, in 1810, was the first bull ever to fetch 1,000 guineas. Its skull, leg and rib bones are on show in Darlington Museum.

Victorian Darlington - The C19th

The C19th saw the country market town with **woollen, leather and linen industries** develop into a major **iron, railway and engineering centre**, and spread from its medieval confines into the surrounding countryside.

The decline of handloom linen weaving and the demise of the machine-spinning linen thread factories was offset by the rise of the woollen industry.

Its development began with **Edward Pease** who came to Darlington in the mid-C18th, entered and then succeeded to his uncle's wool combing business and founded the family firm of Pease. The early mill by the Skerne at the foot of Priestgate organised a domestic industry. It sorted and washed fleeces, distributed the wool in turn to wool combers, spinners and weavers in their cottages and marketed their products. Gradually, machinery was introduced, and it became a factory industry.

The mill was extended in stages. **Low Mill** across the Skerne from St Cuthbert's and **Northgate Weaving Sheds** (Railway Mill) were established, with wool warehouses near Low Mill and at Haughton Road. A fire at Low Mill in 1817 throwing five hundred people out of work illustrates the scale of operations and the importance of the woollen industry to the town. The first **coat of arms** of the new Municipal Borough in 1867 included three bales of wool, acknowledging the industry's status. In the 1880s the firm of **Henry Pease & Co. Ltd.**, as it had by then become known, employed over a thousand people.

The Almshouses behind Skinnergate, Darlington

BEFORE THE FIRST WORLD WAR, a large proportion of its goods went to Germany. In the 1920s the firm was bought by **Lister & Co. Ltd.** of Bradford and closed in 1972, having lasted for two hundred and twenty years. It made material for men's suits and coats and ladies' costumes, blankets, braid, flags and nuns' veiling.

Carpet making was also carried on beside the Skerne behind Northgate by **J. and F. Kipling.** For a while, the Peases made cotton goods. Optical glass-making and the grinding and polishing of spectacles was also a short-lived industry. Leather making continued, and included chamois leather, harness and gloves, ending only when the last currier died between the two World Wars.

During the century Darlington acquired its own gas, water and electricity works. Gas was first manufactured around 1818 by **Edward Todhunter**, a plumber, glazier and tinplate worker of Tubwell Row, to light his own shop, at which crowds gazed in wonder. A Gas Company was formed in 1832, followed in 1849 by the Darlington Gas and Water Company, taken over by the town in 1854. Tees water was said to promote health and religion, and make better beer and tea. The Electricity Works were established in 1900 east of the Skerne, for light, power and trams.

Victorian Growth

THE EARLY C19TH saw buildings beginning to spread beyond the medieval core. By 1826 the first detailed map shows growth along the main roads, a few Georgian terraces, early villas on the fringe and housing east of the Skerne.

With the advent of the **Stockton and Darlington Railway** in 1825, terraced housing took growth northward towards the station and railway works. Development of north-south railways beyond the Skerne and the coming of the iron and engineering industries to the Skerne Valley took terraced housing eastward to Bank Top and Albert Hill. By mid-century, the old burgage plots behind High Row and Skinnergate, Tubwell Row, Bondgate and Northgate had been filled up as overcrowded courts and yards.

FROM THE 1870s, fine terraces of large Victorian and Edwardian houses grew to the west and south of the town centre, and beyond them villas and impressive mansions in parklands, reflecting the town's overall prosperity.

The population of over 5,000 in 1801 grew steadily to over 16,000 in 1861. It nearly doubled in the 1860s, and grew rapidly for the rest of the century. By 1901 it was almost 50,000, and by 1951 almost 85,000, after which it remained fairly stationary. In 1974, the reorganisation of local government brought Darlington Rural District into the Borough and took the total population to around 98,000.

Birthplace of the Railways

The World's First Steam-Hauled Public Railway

Between 1767 and 1818, various schemes were proposed for a canal to carry coal from the south-west Durham pits to the Tees at Stockton. Promoters became convinced that a railway was the solution. **Edward Pease** put a Bill before Parliament for a public railway with rights of way negotiated from the landowners to be affected. Their opposition brought defeat. **George Stephenson's** advice was sought on a revised route.

An Act, delayed by the death of King George III, was passed in 1821. Finance from private subscribers, especially those in the Quaker Community, was made up by Edward Pease, and the project became nicknamed '**The Quaker Railway**'. A Stockton and Darlington Railway Company seal was adopted, inscribed '**Periculum Privatum, Utilitas Publica**' (private risk, public service).

The line from Witton Park Colliery to Stockton via Darlington was for the carriage of coal, iron, lime, corn and other items, and was to be open for use by the public on payment of approved rates. At this stage, horse-drawn transport was intended. A visit by George Stephenson to Edward Pease at his home in Northgate followed by a visit by Pease to see Stephenson's engine at work at Killingworth Colliery persuaded Pease that **steam traction** was better. An amended Act of 1823 provided for steam locomotives and the carrying of passengers.

GEORGE STEPHENSON, appointed engineer to the Company, made a detailed survey for the exact route. He recommended iron rails, to be laid at the 4' 8½" guage already adopted at Killingworth Colliery and copied from carts used on roads. This was to become the world's standard guage. At **Brusselton Incline** a fixed engine designed by George's son Robert was to be used.

STEPHENSON'S 'LOCOMOTION' headed the opening day procession of the **Stockton and Darlington Railway**, the world's first public railway, on **27th September, 1825**. Driven by George Stephenson, 'Locomotion' led a train of thirty-four waggons; six of coal and flour, a coach for the directors and friends, twenty-one waggons fitted with passenger seats for the occasion, and six laden coal waggons. The Darlington artist **John Dobbin's painting** of the occasion as seen from North Road and featuring Ignatius Bonomi's handsome stone bridge over the Skerne is well known. Six hundred passengers continued the journey to Stockton, averaging 10-12 miles (16-20 kms) per hour and reaching up to 15 miles (24 kms) per hour.

'**Locomotion**', in use until 1841, is now housed in **Darlington Railway Centre and Museum** at North Road Station, together with '**Derwent**' designed by **Alfred Kitching** for the S&DR in 1845.

The price of coal transport fell dramatically. The Company continued the line over the Tees in 1831 to the new town and port of **Middlesbrough**. Passenger traffic was at first let out to carriers, and used horse-drawn carriages like stage coaches on flanged wheels. From 1833 it was run by the Company.

FROM ABOUT 1841, wooden sleepers took the place of stone blocks to hold the rails. The first Darlington station was a goods warehouse converted into a booking office and waiting room. It served from 1833 on the east side of North Road, and was replaced in 1842 by the present North Road Station on the west side.

The 'Derwent' at Darlington Railway Centre

S&DR lines ramified into **Teesdale** and **Weardale**, over **Stainmore** and eastward to **Saltburn** to a total of about 200 miles (320 kms). The Company amalgamated with the **North Eastern Railway** in 1863.

Industry Past & Present

A Railway Town

IN THE C19TH railway and general engineering grew and thrived. Soon after the opening of the **Stockton and Darlington Railway** (1825), **Kitching's Foundry** made railway equipment at a site beside North Road Station. Later, railway engines were designed there, including '**Derwent**'. The firm moved on to structural engineering and, as **Whessoe**, made pressure vessels for the gas, oil and nuclear power industries, eventually employing around two thousand people.

The world famous 'Locomotion'

IN THE MID-CENTURY, after the main line railway was established, iron foundries set up in the Skerne Valley around Albert Hill went on to trade with many parts of the world, especially with the spread of the railways overseas. A number of firms made railway equipment including rails. **Darlington Forge** (1853) came to serve the general, marine and electrical engineering industries. By the 1890s, it employed about eight hundred men on its 12 hectare (30 acre) site. Its massive forgings went into famous steamships and warships - Aquitania, Mauritania, Queen Mary, George V, Nelson, Indomitable and large fleet carriers of the Illustrious class. **Summerson's Foundries** made railway switches, sidings and crossings.

In 1863 came **Darlington Railway Locomotive Works** (North Road Shops) to make, repair and overhaul engines for the North Eastern Railway Co. Its 11 hectares (27 acres) of sidings, machine shops, steam hammers, brass and copper foundries and its 200 metres long erecting shops with travelling cranes became the town's largest works, employing nearly three and a half thousand men. Later came **Stooperdale Boiler Shops** and **Faverdale Waggon Works**.

Rise Carr Rolling Mills (1868) became in 1928 **Darlington and Simpson Rolling Mills**, employing over a thousand and making steel sections for collieries, the motor industry and the building trade. **W. Richardson & Co.** (1866) heating engineers made greenhouses and conservatories and industrial heating systems. **Cleveland Bridge and Engineering Co.** (1878) specialised in steel bridges, including the Zambesi, Ganges and Tyne High Level bridges.

In 1901, Robert Stephenson and Hawthorne, transferred their engine building to Darlington at **Springfield Works**, eventually making diesel and diesel-electric locomotives for many parts of the developing world, with a workforce of about nine hundred.

Diversification

DARLINGTON'S GOOD COMMUNICATIONS and fine countryside enabled it to attract new industry in the C20th. In 1927 came the chemical and insulating company, **Darchem**, processing local dolomite (magnesian limestone) for industrial insulation and for use in printing, plastics and synthetic rubber, ceramics, glass and toiletries. After the Second World War, in 1947, two firms offering opportunities for women set up. **Paton and Baldwin's** made knitting yarns employing over a thousand workers, whilst **Alexander** made men's clothing, employing over five hundred.

The early 1960s, however, brought a traumatic closure of the railway shops and allied works and the loss of several thousand jobs. Later on, even the woollen industry was to end with the closure of Pease's mill, Paton's factory and Alexander's. These, however, gave an opportunity for new industries to arrive. The **Teachers' Pensions** section of the **Department of Education and Science** brought clerical work. Industrial estates at Faverdale, North Road and Yarm Road, attracted modern works: **Bowater Containers** for packaging, **Chrysler-Cummins** diesel engines, **Cummins** injection system, **Torrington** bearings, **Carreras Rothmans** cigarettes and most recently **Hutchison Telecom** business and personal telecommunications.

Famous People

LEWIS CARROLL (1832-1898) of 'Alice in Wonderland' fame, was Charles Lutwidge Dodgson, eldest son of the Venerable Charles Dodgson, Rector of Croft 1843-1868. From the age of eleven, Croft Rectory was his home for twenty-five years until the death of his father in 1868. During this time, one of eleven children, he devised games and entertainment for the young family. He wrote and sketched plays, stories and family magazines. His talents developed at Croft and the origin and inspiration for his humorous writings whilst an Oxford don are believed to lie in the North.

His animals may originate with carvings on the sedilia in Croft Church. 'Jabberwocky' could have been triggered by the local legend of the Sockburn Worm and its representation on the arms of the Conyers family whose ancestor slew the beastly serpent. At Ripon Cathedral, animal carvings on the stalls include monsters, a rabbit and a turtle. Beverley, where Charles spent several vacations, claims that the white rabbit was based on a peculiar hare on the church door. Another candidate is Sunderland with a walrus in the Museum and ships' carpenters in plenty. Charles often visited his relatives in nearby Whitburn, where in verse competitions most of 'Jabberwocky' was written.

Lewis Carroll is remembered by a plaque in St Peter's Church, Croft, and by a mural in Darlington District Library.

The Quakers

Quakers settled in Darlington from the C17th onwards. Engaged in shopkeeping, industry and trade, by the C19th they assumed an influence out of all proportion to their numbers. They came to dominate local government and town affairs, providing half of the first Board of Health, a dozen Mayors of the new Victorian Municipal Borough, and many MPs. Only a few prominent Quakers can be mentioned here.

The Backhouses and Peases were both outstandingly influential and established family dynasties. Arriving in Darlington in the mid- C18th, they worked first in linens and woollens, moving later into banking, railways, coal mining, ironstone mining, quarrying, coke and brick making and water undertakings. As promoters and investors, they made great wealth, built early villas in the suburbs surpassed from the 1860s by their palatial mansions in parkland settings. They worked for educational and social welfare in the town and region.

JAMES BACKHOUSE (1721-1798) of West Lodge and his son Jonathan (1747-1826) together founded Backhouse's Bank in 1774 in Northgate, moving later to High Row. Branches and agencies were established in the main towns of the region. Until its merger with Barclay & Co. in 1896, all seventeen partners were Backhouses. The last Backhouse partner served until 1973.

JONATHAN BACKHOUSE (1779-1842) of Polam, was treasurer and shares promoter for establishing the Stockton & Darlington Railway. He won a Royal Society of Arts medal in 1813 for tree planting on his Weardale and Lanchester estates.

EDWARD PEASE (1767-1858) was a merchant in the family woollen firm whose Darlington mills in 1816 employed six hundred. From middle life he concentrated on establishing what became in 1825 the Stockton and Darlington Railway, the world's first public railway for goods and passengers, for which he was called 'The Father of Railways'. A visit to his Northgate home from George Stephenson, engine wright at Killinghall Colliery, convinced him to adopt steam haulage. The last of the plain Quakers of Darlington, he was troubled that wealth was diverting his family from the simple life of members of the religious Society of Friends.

JOSEPH PEASE (1799-1872) of Southend, second son of Edward, trained in the woollen firm, became the first and life-long treasurer of the S&DR, which he extended across the Tees at Stockton to Port Darlington coal staithes. He was also chief partner in the Middlesbrough Estate Co. which bought land to establish a new town for five thousand. Joseph was the first ever Quaker MP, serving for South Durham after the Great Reform Act of 1832.

HENRY PEASE (1807-1881) of Pierremont, younger brother of Joseph, trained in the leather industry and became the first Mayor of Darlington, and MP for South Durham 1857-1865. He was a promoter of railways, the Middlesbrough and Guisborough, the Darlington to Barnard Castle, the Stainmore Line to Kirkby Stephen and Tebay with the famous Belah Viaduct and the extension of the

S&DR beyond Redcar to Saltburn, which he developed as a new seaside resort and gardens. In 1875, Henry presided at the Golden Jubilee celebrations in Darlington of the S&DR, being the last survivor of the founding pioneers.

SIR JOSEPH WHITWELL PEASE (1828-1903), of The Woodlands and later of Hutton Hall, eldest son of Joseph Pease, was the head of **Pease and Partners**, director of the S&DR, on the Board of the NER, chairman of the Tees Conservancy Commission and President of the Peace Society. He was **MP for South Durham** and for the **Barnard Castle Division**, serving for thirty-five years, and was **knighted in 1882**, the first Darlington Quaker to accept a title. He was especially praised for his efforts in extending the Weardale railway beyond Stanhope to Wearhead and for 'workmen's tickets' to help to keep mines and quarries working.

SIR DAVID DALE (1829-1906) of **West Lodge** was a conciliator, an authority on industrial arbitration, and served on three Royal Commissions, on Trade, Mining Royalties and Labour. He was related to David Dale, founder of New Lanark Mills, and to Robert Owen, social reformer.

JOHN FOWLER (1826-1864) married **Lucy Pease**, one of Joseph's daughters. In 1856 he invented the steam plough, winning the Royal Agriculture Society's £500 Award with a plough built by Robert Stephenson's Newcastle works. South Park has a Fowler memorial.

JOHN KENDREW (1752-1800), a weaver, invented a machine for grinding spectacles and optical instruments, and set up a mill on the Skerne.

Others of Note - A Selection

WILLIAM EMERSON (1701-1782) of Hurworth, was a well known mathematician with twenty-five published works, the best known being '**Fluxions**'. He secretly wrote for a ladies' magazine, and wore eccentric clothes, some from material spun by his wife and woven in the village.

BISHOP WILLIAM HOGARTH (1786-1866) taught at Ushaw College and made Darlington his home as Roman Catholic parish priest from 1821. He became also the **Roman Catholic Bishop of Hexham** in 1850 and later of **Newcastle**.

WILLIAM BEWICK (1795-1866) was born at Haughton-le-Skerne where he also spent his last twenty-two years. An artist, he became a copier of old masters and a portrait painter. His drawings of the Elgin marbles and copying of Michelangelo's frescoes in the Sistine Chapel were praised.

The 1875 Statue of Joseph Pease in High Row

LIEUT-GENERAL SIR HENRY MARSHMAN HAVELOCK-ALLAN, Bart., VC, KCB., MP (1830-1897), served with his father in the **Indian Mutiny** at the siege of Cawnpore and at Lucknow where he won the Victoria Cross. In 1880 he inherited Blackwell Grange and adopted the name of Allan. He was killed at the Khyber Pass.

W. T. STEAD (1849-1912) was editor of the **Northern Echo** 1871-1880, a campaigning journalist and prominent publicist. He later edited the **Pall Mall Gazette** in London in the 1880s, running an anti-vice crusade, founded other publications and died in the Titanic disaster.

IGNATIUS TIMOTHY TREBITCH LINCOLN (1879-1943), a Hungarian Jew who emigrated, narrowly beat Herbert Pike Pease to be **MP for Darlington** in January 1910. Losing money, he withdrew from the November election, was charged with forgery in America in 1915, suspected of being a German spy, deported from Britain, travelled, was advisor to Chinese warlords, and in Ceylon, became a Buddhist and later a monk.

THE FOUR BRADFORD BROTHERS won military honours, including two VCs in the First World War, which only one of them survived.

Some Notable Buildings

Buildings of architectural and historical interest outside the town centre abound, and many are Listed. Churches sprang up as the town expanded. Farmland was built over, first by villas and mansions with parklands, later as pleasant suburbs. Some of the mansions survived the process. The following is a personal choice of buildings grouped in turn along the main roads out of town.

DARLINGTON CIVIC THEATRE in Parkgate, opened in 1907 as the **New Hippodrome and Palace of Varieties**. It was G. G. Hoskins' last major building. Managed by **Signor Pepi**, this period Edwardian theatre in red brick and orange terracotta seated over a thousand persons and attracted the well-known theatre personalities of the day. Bought by Darlington Borough Council in 1964, retrenchment, improvements and success culminated in expansion and refurbishment in 1990 to seat and refresh nine hundred in comfort. On reopening, the Mayor, Councillor Eric Roberts, called the theatre one of the town's most precious assets, the jewel in the crown.

BANK TOP STATION was built for the North Eastern Railway in 1887 by **William Bell**, when the S&DR route was diverted via Geneva junction. Its curving, double span, iron-framed roof rests on columns which embrace the insignia of related companies. An Italianate clock tower terminates Victoria Road. The North Eastern Hotel (now The Coachman) catered for passengers.

THE MEAD off Yarm Road, was Darlington's first **Garden Suburb**, approved in 1912. Its pebble dashed semi-detached villas stand in gardens with privet hedges in a grass-verged, tree-lined crescent.

ST ANDREW'S CHURCH in Haughton-le-Skerne is Norman, and even older than St Cuthbert's. Its narrow, aisleless nave, chancel and massive tower were built between 1130 and 1150. The transepts, vestry and porch were added in 1895. The interior is notable for its C17th panelling, pews, pulpit, reading desks and stalls for clergy and choir. **Butler House**, the old rectory, has C18th brick wings to an ancient stone core with an exposed medieval window.

ST AUGUSTINE'S RC CHURCH hides in a small precinct in Coniscliffe Road. Built in 1826, before the Catholic Emancipation Act, it was designed by **Ignatius Bonomi**, with later alterations by **Joseph Aloysius Hansom**.

ELM RIDGE is a fine stone mansion built in 1867 for **John and Sophia Pease,** by **Hoskins**. For half a century it was the home of their daughter **Mary Anna Hodgkin**, and it is now a Methodist church.

BROKEN SCAR PUMPING STATION houses a steam-driven beam engine of 1904. Darlington waterworks began abstracting from the Tees in 1849. Steam pumping, filtration processes and a 1913 gas engine are working exhibits.

SOUTHEND along Grange Road, formerly a Roman Catholic convent and now the Grange Hotel, was the much enlarged home of **Joseph Pease**, industrialist, railway promoter and co-founder in 1830 of Middlesbrough new town.

POLAM HALL is a villa of 1795 enlarged by banker **Jonathan Backhouse** and his wife, a Quaker minister. Jonathan expanded the grounds by the Skerne and created a lake. From 1854 Polam became a boarding school for young ladies.

HAREWOOD GROVE was built by **John Green** of Newcastle in the 1840s, and is an elegant, Grade II* listed terrace of eight houses, now flats, with a pediment, pilasters and a long cast-iron balcony.

BLACKWELL GRANGE built by **George Allan**, merchant, in 1710, has a south wing of 1717. A matching extension was by **Sir Henry Marshman Havelock Allan** in 1889. A Grade II* listed building, it has been extended as a hotel with wide views in a parkland golf course.

Moving from Bondgate towards Woodland Road, note **Bondgate Methodist Church**, in Salt Yard, off Bondgate, a Grade II* listed building of 1812, by W. Sherwood. It has a pleasing doorway with a radiating fanlight.

WEST LODGE West Crescent, was begun by **James Backhouse**, founder of the bank. **Thomas Backhouse**, retired chairman of Lloyds Shipping Insurance, gave it a new front with a pediment and pavilions in 1803. Sir David Dale's later embellishments included a grand portico.

THE WOODLANDS began in 1815 as a small villa. **Joseph Whitwell Pease**, eldest son of Joseph Pease, later knighted, doubled it in size in 1860 and added a fashionable tower, to designs by Richardson and Ross.

PIERREMONT Tower Road, began in the 1830s as a villa for **John Botcherby**, whose initial appears on a stained glass window by **Wailes** of Newcastle. Vast Tudor Gothic additions by **Henry Pease** to this first villa of stone in Darlington culminated in 1874 with a stone conservatory, sunken garden, carriage entrance arch and clock tower designed by **Alfred Waterhouse**, ready for the Golden Jubilee of the S&DR. Pierremont was nicknamed the Buckingham Palace of Darlington!

Long garden walls and gate piers mark the sites of numerous villas and mansions, parks and gardens along **Woodland Road** and **Carmel Road**.

MOWDEN was the last mansion inside the old Borough boundary, built in 1881, in Staindrop Road, by **Alfred Waterhouse**, for **Edwin Lucas Pease**. It is of Domestic style in red brick, tile and terracotta, now a pensions offices.

ALONG CARMEL ROAD are **Thornfield**, 1859, in red brick Gothic built for **John Marley**, mining engineer; and **Grantley**, 1899, by **G.G. Hoskins** built for solicitor **G.N. Watson**. The long stone and brick walls on the west side enclosed the park of an C18th villa converted into **Carmel Convent** in 1830, with a chapel of 1854 by **George Goldie**. In red brick Gothic, **St Clare's Abbey** by **J.& C. Hansom** came into the park in 1858. **Danesmoor**, 1886 by **William Bell** built for solicitor **Edward Wooler**, has a cast iron verandah.

TWO 1860s MANSIONS in Pease's cream brick with red sandstone dressings by Alfred Waterhouse could be reached via Hummersknott Avenue and The Headlands. **Uplands** built for **Rachael Pease** was demolished, but **Hummersknott** built for **Arthur Pease** is now Carmel School. Pease developed a 105 hectare (260 acre) park whose mature trees and copses adorn the later suburban estates. The first Royal Agricultural Show in County Durham was held here.

DOWN NUNNERY LANE on Wilton Drive, stands **Wilton House** built in the 1860s for **Ann Allan** on farmlands then owned by the Allans of Blackwell. Nearby is **Hill Close House**, a former farmhouse with a C15th core to a mainly C17th house of cobble, rubble and brick. It has C18th sash windows and blocked remnants of stone mullioned windows. Below, and still cultivated, is **Hummersknott Garden**, the last of the numerous kitchen gardens of Darlington. From its railed west entrance can be seen the oldest house inside the old Borough boundary.

146 NORTHGATE is Edward Pease's House to which George Stephenson came to propose steam power for the S&DR. There is a plaque on the altered front. In his day it was backed by orchards across the valley of the Skerne. Opposite is the old **Technical College**, 1897, by **G.G. Hoskins**, in extravagant style, which was built in the grounds of Elmfield, William Backhouse's villa. So was elegant bow-windowed **North Lodge**, 1833, for **John Beaumont Pease**, now the Teachers' Centre. In 1901, the grounds became North Lodge Park where the Bandstand was soon erected.

NORTH ROAD STATION off High Northgate, reached via Station Road, dates from 1842 and is believably Britain's oldest station still in railway use, its cast iron colonnaded centre with balancing wings has a cast iron spiral staircase in the train shed behind. The whole is now a railway museum to the S&DR and the NER, with the original '**Locomotion No. 1**' its star attraction. From John Street can be viewed **Skerne Bridge**, 1824, by **Ignatius Bonomi**, featured in John Dobbin's famous painting of the opening day of the S&DR.

The Old Town Hall and newly-restored Market Cross

DUKE STREET AND ABBEY ROAD developed from the 1870s right through to the 1960s, at first as town terraced houses, with more ambitious terraces to follow along Stanhope Road. In 1875, the **Grammar School of Queen Elizabeth** moved to a new building by **G.G. Hoskins** in Vane Terrace. It had an undercroft playground, later filled in, and took boarders. Next door, the Victorian Gothic red brick **North of England Training College of the British and Foreign Schools Society** by **J.P. Pritchett** was opened in 1876. Greatly expanded after World War II, when it also took men and mature students, it closed in 1978. Abbey Road acquired fine early C19th villas.

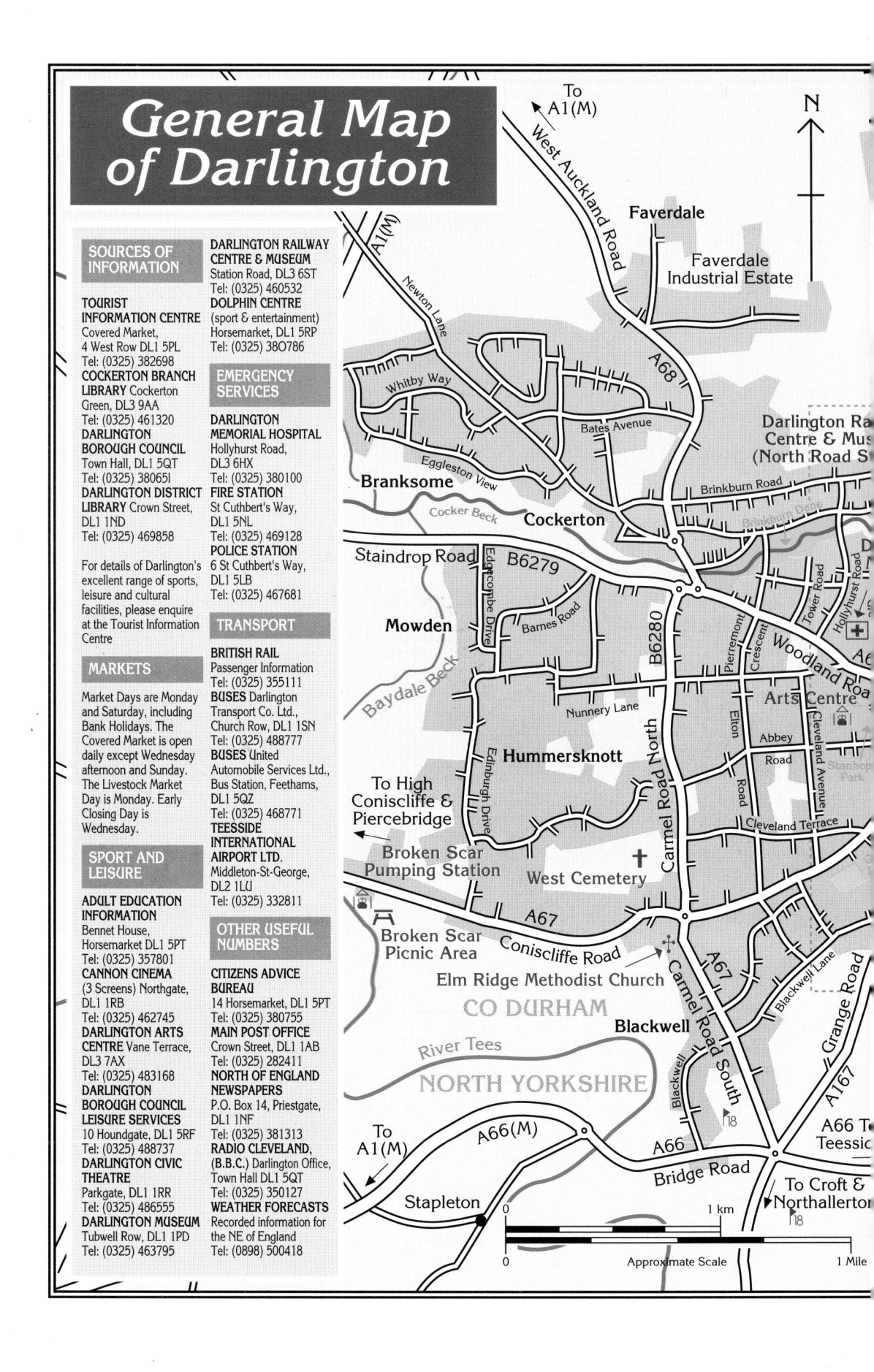

General Map of Darlington

SOURCES OF INFORMATION

TOURIST INFORMATION CENTRE
Covered Market,
4 West Row DL1 5PL
Tel: (0325) 382698
COCKERTON BRANCH LIBRARY Cockerton
Green, DL3 9AA
Tel: (0325) 461320
DARLINGTON BOROUGH COUNCIL
Town Hall, DL1 5QT
Tel: (0325) 380651
DARLINGTON DISTRICT LIBRARY Crown Street,
DL1 1ND
Tel: (0325) 469858

For details of Darlington's excellent range of sports, leisure and cultural facilities, please enquire at the Tourist Information Centre

MARKETS

Market Days are Monday and Saturday, including Bank Holidays. The Covered Market is open daily except Wednesday afternoon and Sunday. The Livestock Market Day is Monday. Early Closing Day is Wednesday.

SPORT AND LEISURE

ADULT EDUCATION INFORMATION
Bennet House,
Horsemarket DL1 5PT
Tel: (0325) 357801
CANNON CINEMA
(3 Screens) Northgate,
DL1 1RB
Tel: (0325) 462745
DARLINGTON ARTS CENTRE Vane Terrace,
DL3 7AX
Tel: (0325) 483168
DARLINGTON BOROUGH COUNCIL LEISURE SERVICES
10 Houndgate, DL1 5RF
Tel: (0325) 488737
DARLINGTON CIVIC THEATRE
Parkgate, DL1 1RR
Tel: (0325) 486555
DARLINGTON MUSEUM
Tubwell Row, DL1 1PD
Tel: (0325) 463795

DARLINGTON RAILWAY CENTRE & MUSEUM
Station Road, DL3 6ST
Tel: (0325) 460532
DOLPHIN CENTRE
(sport & entertainment)
Horsemarket, DL1 5RP
Tel: (0325) 380786

EMERGENCY SERVICES

DARLINGTON MEMORIAL HOSPITAL
Hollyhurst Road,
DL3 6HX
Tel: (0325) 380100
FIRE STATION
St Cuthbert's Way,
DL1 5NL
Tel: (0325) 469128
POLICE STATION
6 St Cuthbert's Way,
DL1 5LB
Tel: (0325) 467681

TRANSPORT

BRITISH RAIL
Passenger Information
Tel: (0325) 355111
BUSES Darlington
Transport Co. Ltd.,
Church Row, DL1 1SN
Tel: (0325) 488777
BUSES United
Automobile Services Ltd.,
Bus Station, Feethams,
DL1 5QZ
Tel: (0325) 468771
TEESSIDE INTERNATIONAL AIRPORT LTD.
Middleton-St-George,
DL2 1LU
Tel: (0325) 332811

OTHER USEFUL NUMBERS

CITIZENS ADVICE BUREAU
14 Horsemarket, DL1 5PT
Tel: (0325) 380755
MAIN POST OFFICE
Crown Street, DL1 1AB
Tel: (0325) 282411
NORTH OF ENGLAND NEWSPAPERS
P.O. Box 14, Priestgate,
DL1 1NF
Tel: (0325) 381313
RADIO CLEVELAND,
(B.B.C.) Darlington Office,
Town Hall DL1 5QT
Tel: (0325) 350127
WEATHER FORECASTS
Recorded information for the NE of England
Tel: (0898) 500418

To A1(M)

N

Faverdale

Faverdale Industrial Estate

West Auckland Road

Newton Lane

A68

Whitby Way

Bates Avenue

Eggleston View

Branksome

Cocker Beck

Cockerton

Darlington Ra Centre & Mus (North Road St

Brinkburn Road

Brinkburn Dene

Staindrop Road

B6279

Edgecombe Drive

Mowden

Barnes Road

B6280

Pierremont

Crescent

Tower Road

Hollyhurst Road

Woodland Roa

A6

Baydale Beck

Nunnery Lane

Elton

Arts Centre

Abbey Road

Cleveland Avenue

Stanhop Park

Hummersknott

Edinburgh Drive

Carmel Road North

To High Coniscliffe & Piercebridge

Cleveland Terrace

Broken Scar Pumping Station

West Cemetery

A67

Broken Scar Picnic Area

Coniscliffe Road

Carmel Road South

A67

Blackwell Lane

Grange Road

Elm Ridge Methodist Church

CO DURHAM

Blackwell

River Tees

NORTH YORKSHIRE

Blackwell

A167

To A1(M)

A66(M)

A66

Bridge Road

A66 To Teessic

To Croft & Northallerton

Stapleton

0   1 km

0   Approximate Scale   1 Mile

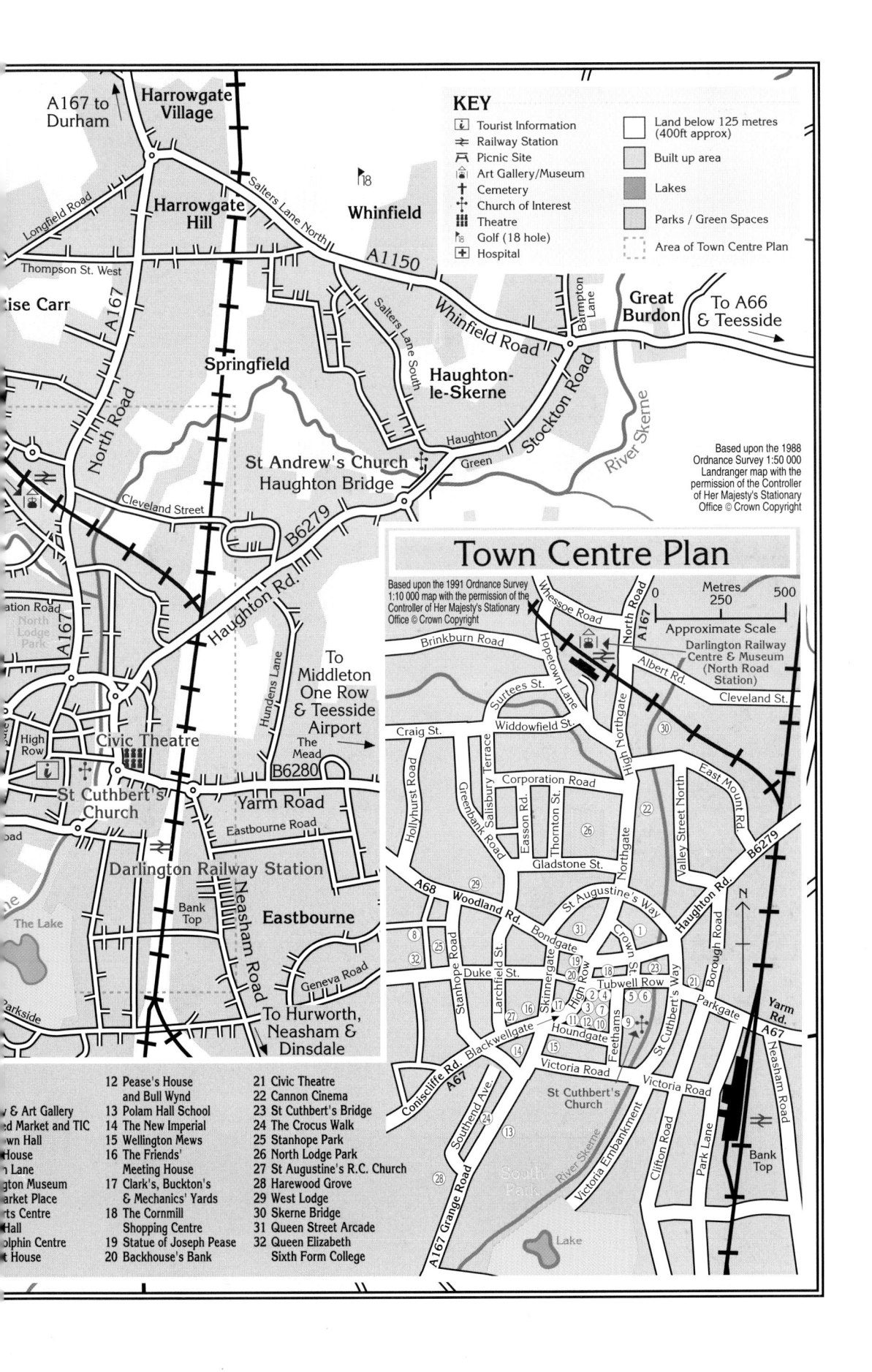

St Cuthbert's Church

THE PARISH CHURCH OF ST CUTHBERT, Darlington, is one of the most important buildings in the county. Begun by **Hugh Pudsey, Bishop of Durham** 1153-1195, it was a collegiate church with a vicar and four canons or prebends supported by property in Priestgate and Prebends' Row. It ranked next to Durham Cathedral. The processional west door marked its status. In 1439, **Bishop Neville** promoted the vicar to a dean. Two chantries, of **Mary the Virgin** and of **All Saints**, were founded in the C13th and C16th.

AT THE REFORMATION, however, the chantries were suppressed and the college of canons or prebends dissolved. St Cuthbert's became a parish church with a vicar. The ancient parish included Darlington Borough and Bondgate, Cockerton, Blackwell and Archdeacon Newton.

Darlington's splendid St Cuthbert's Church

The present building, the first in Durham in the **Early English Gothic** style, was begun soon after 1180. Pointed arches and a plethora of narrow lancet windows, single and grouped, stepped and in arcades, are its joyous hallmark, enhanced by steep soaring roofs. The plan is cruciform, with a nave, chancel, and transepts of the same height and a crossing tower unique amongst early Durham churches. At first without aisles or a spire, the aisles with lancet windows came soon

afterwards. Work was probably completed by the early C13th.

IN THE EARLY C14TH the low, squat tower gained a belfry with four bells and a slender stone spire, one of only five medieval spires in the county. However, the extra weight caused subsidence and a westerly thrust, still seen today in the leaning west front. To remedy this, windows and arcades were blocked, and a reinforcing bridge with strong ribs was built across the chancel arch. This unique stone bridge served as a rood screen and later supported the organ. In the C14th, too, the aisle roofs were raised and two-light windows in the Decorated style replaced the original lancets.

The spire was struck by lightning in 1750. When rebuilt, the spire was shortened, and the angle moulding and lights were omitted from its upper reaches. The present clock by **Potts of Leeds** dates from 1909.

IN 1862-65 SIR GEORGE GILBERT SCOTT carried out a major restoration of the nave and tower. Flat ceilings, galleries and box pews inserted in the C18th were removed from the transepts, nave and aisles, and a pulpit of Scott's design put in. **J.P. Pritchett** restored the chancel in 1864-65. During these operations, fragments of Saxon crosses, a Danish tombstone and the foundations of an earlier church were found. Scott, a specialist in church architecture, regarded St Cuthbert's as one of the most beautiful and most uniform in style of any he knew.

Since Darlington belonged to the Bishop until the mid-C19th, there are no early tombs or memorials to landed families. **Recent memorials** include those to the Allan family of Blackwell, to Lieutenant General Sir Henry Havelock Allan and to Brigadier General Roland Boys Bradford. **The original font** has a base of Frosterley marble, with a stone bowl of around 1375. Its soaring carved oak font cover four stages high, in elaborate Bishop Cosin Gothic style, dates from 1662.

NOTEWORTHY IN THE CHANCEL are the C14th sedilia. The C15th carved oak chancel stalls for the college of clergy date from the time of **Cardinal Langley** (1406-37). His eagle appears on one. Carved misericords beneath the seats feature faces, men in boots, monsters, birds, and angels. The C16th **Easter Sepulchre** is a rare feature, one of only two in the diocese. A mosaic reredos by **John Dobbin** depicts the Last Supper.

The Town Centre Trail

The Streets of the Town Centre

After the Second World War the **Darlington Inner Ring Road**, approved in the 1952 Development Plan, was constructed in stages. Property was demolished beyond the River Skerne, behind Northgate and Bondgate, and along one side of Victoria Road. Darlington Borough Council built St Cuthbert's Way and St Augustine's Way between 1969 and 1974, while Durham County Council made Victoria Road into a dual carriageway by 1977. After a Public Inquiry, it was decided in 1990 not to build the last section. This would have completed the ring by going along Larchfield Street and behind Skinnergate to join up with the end of St Cuthbert's Way.

The line of the ring road encloses the present town centre and main shopping area. It also roughly defines the area of the medieval town, the Borough with Bondgate. In the centre is the ancient **Market Place** from which radiate the main streets - **Northgate, Blackwellgate, Tubwell Row**, and **Bondgate**. These lead outwards to North Road, Woodland Road, Coniscliffe Road, Grange Road, Parkgate, Yarm Road and Haughton Road, like a spider's web.

HIGH ROW was formerly called Headrow. High Row, Horsemarket and Tubwell Row face Market Place. Behind them stretch former **medieval burgage plots** ending in back lanes which developed into Skinnergate, Houndgate and Priestgate.

Connecting Market Place with the back lanes are **Bull Wynd**, formerly much narrower, and **Post House Wynd** which has been pedestrianised. 'Wynd' is an old North Country word for a narrow lane or street. Post House Wynd is named after a posting house, the Talbot Inn, whose stable yard arch can still be seen near the High Row end. Previously the Wynd had been known as Glover's Wynd and Charegate, 'chare' also being an old North Country word.

The burgage plots were built over in the C18th and C19th as **Yards**, as were also the rear plots behind Bondgate and other town centre streets. Rights of way through some of the

Yards give short cuts for pedestrians, like Chancery Lane, Clark's Yard, Mechanics' Yard and Russell's Yard.

Bakehouse Hill was an C18th encroachment on to the Market Place. One flank faces Church Row. The other flank is named East Row. The **Covered Market and old Town Hall**, built in 1864, impinge upon a much larger area of the ancient Market Place than their predecessors, the tollbooth and shambles. The west flank of the Covered Market, a former open canopy now filled in with shops, is named West Row.

Two footways lead off the east side of Market Place on either side of **St Cuthbert's Church**. Church Lane zig-zags behind the former vicarage to Tubwell Row, whilst a way through the Town Hall grounds crosses the River Skerne by a footbridge.

BONDGATE was where the Bishop's bond tenants lived. **Prebends Row** had property in it whose income helped to support the prebends in St Cuthbert's Church. **Tubwell Row** was presumably named after the Tubwell, a public source of water. **Feethams** evolved from a small lane which led to the Fetholmes, fertile floodable meadows beside the Skerne.

High Row, Covered Market and the Town Clock

NORTHGATE, formerly Duresmegate, the Durham Road, was part of the Great North Road or the Post Road from Edinburgh to London. This came via York and Croft Bridge, Grange Road and Blackwellgate into Market Place and out via Northgate and North Road to Durham. In 1745 the route became the **Boroughbridge to Durham Road**, the first turnpike road in County Durham. Later it became part of the A1. Its queues of traffic were relieved in 1965 by the building of the **Darlington Bypass** along the line of the old Merrybent Railway. The Bypass later developed into the Durham Motorway.

CROWN STREET was newly made in the mid-C19th, and **Victoria Road** in the late 1860s after the building of **Bank Top Station**. **Duke Street** developed from the 1870s on land owned by the Duke of Cleveland, a member of the Vane Family of Raby Castle. Barnard, Powlett, Raby and Winston Streets, Stanhope Road, Vane Terrace, Cleveland Avenue and Cleveland Terrace are all street names derived from his family and estates. The **Queen Street Arcade**, opened in 1968, replaces a nearby Queen Street of Queen Victoria's reign.

Town Centre Buildings - A Town Trail

MARKET PLACE was probably laid out in the late C12th when **Bishop Pudsey** established his chartered Borough, and built a new church and manor house in Darlington. Market Place was very spacious until buildings encroached as islands in the centre. It is still large. A scheme to replace the old Town Hall and Covered Market in the 1960s by a large covered shopping centre occupying much of the open market area was abandoned. Most of the surrounding buildings have now been renovated, whilst enhancement of the open area is under discussion.

THE COVERED MARKET, OLD TOWN HALL AND TOWN CLOCK, 1864, were designed by the famous and prolific architect **Alfred Waterhouse**. They were ready for the founding of the independent Municipal Borough in 1867, whose centenary celebrations were marked by a visit of Queen Elizabeth II and HRH The Duke of Edinburgh. The Italianate clock tower, gift of **Joseph Pease**, has become the symbol of Darlington. The flight of steps facing Market Place was the site of public pronouncements. The cast iron market hall and glazed colonnade, and the buildings in cream brick and sandstone, were renovated in 1979.

DORIC HOUSE, on Tubwell Row, is also a cast iron framed building, with exposed columns and ornate ironwork on the facade. Its mansard roof has circular dormer windows.

CHURCH LANE, behind the Nag's Head, is hemmed in by C17th walls of narrow hand-made brick, belonging to the churchyard on one side and to the old Nag's Head Inn on the other. The latter, demolished in 1963 except for this preserved rear wall, was originally built as a vicarage. Some cobbled walling is also exposed to view.

DARLINGTON MUSEUM is a pleasant red brick and terracotta building ornamented with swags and Dutch gables. Local history, archaeology and natural history are displayed in a modern setting. Souvenirs and publications of local interest are on sale.

ST CUTHBERT'S BRIDGE across the Skerne is an iron bridge with ornate balustrades and attractive lamps. Built in 1895, it replaced an C18th stone bridge whose predecessors were a nine-arched bridge and a three-arched bridge supplemented by stepping stones, a causeway and a ford.

THE SKERNE hereabouts formerly meandered over marshy ground, and widened on the upstream side of the bridge into a pool called **Mill Pot**, where a mill race rejoined the river. The corn mill, Pease's woollen mill and the mill race have all gone. Downstream on the east bank was **Pease's Low Mill**, formerly John Kendrew's optical glass factory and latterly Denham's Foundry. Across the river, **John Wesley** preached in 1761, where a car showroom now stands. This area was Clay Row, and often suffered floods. From 1872, the river has been straightened and embanked in stages over a long distance and flooding eliminated.

Darlington's beautiful South Park

THE IRON FOOTBRIDGE is a vantage point from which to view the attractive landscaping of the river banks, the Town Hall grounds and the churchyard. Mallard nest hereabouts and kingfishers may be seen. Once upon a time, trout, salmon, pike, eels and otters frequented the Skerne. Moorhens, coots and other wildlife can still be seen, especially along its course via

Victoria Embankment, South Park and Polam Hall Grounds.

THE GRAMMAR SCHOOL OF QUEEN ELIZABETH once stood just beyond the bridge end, where a stone plaque marks its site. There may have been a very early grammar school as part of the responsibilities of the collegiate Church of St Cuthbert. A Grammar School and a chantry chapel were founded around 1530 by **Robert Marshall**. Possibly he erected the school building which stood outside the east end of the chancel near the Skerne. After the Reformation, the Grammar School was refounded by a charter granted by Elizabeth I in 1563. In l647, a new school was built on the same site, with a thatched roof later replaced by pantiles. In 1813 a new single storey school was built at the south east corner of the churchyard. It was raised to two storeys in 1846, as recorded on the plaque at the bridge end. The boys moved to a larger new building at Vane Terrace in 1875, but the little C19th building survived until 1950.

DARLINGTON TOWN HALL was opened by HRH Princess Anne (The Princess Royal) in 1970. The luxurious Council Chamber stands separate from the Council Offices, the two linked by a soaring foyer in white marble. The forecourt in front of the lofty grey curtain walling features '**Resurgence**'. This metal sculpture by **John Hoskins** was a gift from Darlington Lions Club to celebrate the recovery of the town after the closure of its railway industries in the 1960s. The Town Hall and grounds are on the site of the C12th courtyard Manor House of Bishop Pudsey, which survived until 1870.

ST CUTHBERT'S CHURCH GROUNDS form a quiet island in the town centre. Mature trees were retained when the churchyard was landscaped in 1971. Lofty beech, lime, oak, maple, ash and silver birch sprinkle the lawns. Younger holly and laburnum add interest, as do the few older gravestones retained. The graveyard was closed for burials in 1857, and **West Cemetery** on Carmel Road was opened. A memorial garden to people buried in the churchyard lies next to a new Church Hall built in 1976 in the north west corner.

ST CUTHBERT'S CHURCH is a large, lofty and elegantly simple Early English cruciform church with steep roofs, a central tower and spire, a long nave and a profusion of grouped lancet windows. Begun around 1180 by **Bishop Pudsey**, its Gothic style, all pre-1250, remains remarkably intact and uniform apart from the C14th aisle windows, upper tower and spire. The vestry of about 1500 has C18th windows

and parapets. The processional west door indicates its status as a collegiate church. Above the door is a replica statue of **St Cuthbert** holding the head of **St Oswald**, Saxon King of Northumbria. On the nave facing south, a sundial inscribed in Latin pleads 'Let the day be without strife'. The upper part of the slender spire, damaged by lightning in 1750, was rebuilt without its angle moulding. The weight of the tower and spire caused sinkage. Reinforcements can be seen on the external corners of the tower, and adjoining windows were blocked as strengthening.

The vivid colours of South Park's floral creations

THE DOLPHIN CENTRE on Horsemarket marks the sites of the Deanery and the Dolphin Inn. Opened in 1983, it was built to the design of Borough Architect **Gabriel Lowes** to fit in with the traditional architecture around the Market Place. Broken up rooflines and facades disguise the huge scale of this modern sports and leisure centre.

BENNET HOUSE, an C18th town house with a Gibbs type door surround, is a Grade II* listed building. Restored in 1975 for Architectural Heritage Year, it caters for Social Services and Adult Education. The Bull Wynd gable was rebuilt last century. The rest of Horsemarket beyond Bull Wynd was rebuilt, preserving the old facades, shop fronts and Chancery Lane.

BULL WYND has two ancient stones set into a wall. One has a relief of a bull with a shovel tail, a crest of the Bulmer family who owned property hereabouts. The other is inscribed 'Anthon Bulmer and Marie Lasinbie'. They were married in 1665. A Bull Inn stood on the site. Behind is **Pease's House** where Edward Pease, 'Father of Railways', once lived. Its paved courtyard can be reached through the archway or via a passage from Horsemarket (when open) or from Chancery Lane. Cobble foundations and walling and the proportions of the house suggest a possible medieval origin.

Exterior features imply renovations in the C18th and C19th. The south front with a heavy door surround and Venetian windows faces its former walled garden, now a **Heritage Garden** with seats and a cast iron fountain brought from Joseph Pease's park to mark the centenary of the publication of the Northern Echo in Darlington. **Central Hall**, 1846, designed by Darlington architect **John Middleton**, was a centre of C19th social life, meetings and events. Later it served as a cinema and recently as the Borough finance department. Beautifully renovated by the Borough Council, it now houses orchestral and chamber concerts, meetings and other events as part of the Dolphin Centre.

HOUNDGATE preserves a fragment of its former C18th and C19th housing where professional people lived and worked. **Selby House** became a Quaker girls' boarding school set up in 1848 by the Proctor sisters Jane, Barbara and Elizabeth of Selby, where Jane had long been a schoolteacher. They moved the school to **Polam Hall** in 1854. In recent years Selby House was the Town Clerk's Office and is now the Registry Office.

THE NEW IMPERIAL on Grange Road corner was built in 1875 for Edward Wooler, a Darlington solicitor, and designed by **Ross and Lamb** as the Trevelyan or New Temperance Hotel. On Queen Victoria's Golden Jubilee in 1887 its name was changed to the Imperial Hotel. It has recently been converted into business units.

GRANGE ROAD is now a specialist shopping area. It first saw building development in the early years of the C19th as houses and businesses began to move away from the town centre. Most of the early premises were rebuilt or altered. **Wellington Mews**, a recent shopping alcove, recalls an earlier building named after the hero of the Battle of Waterloo (1815).

THE NORTH OF ENGLAND SCHOOL FURNISHING Co. is now Lloyds Bank, with offices above. The Company began as a religious tract and bible society by **John Pease** in Northgate, and evolved into school books, stationery and furnishings. The new shop and offices designed by **G.G. Hoskins** with exuberant terracotta ornamentation were opened on the day of Queen Victoria's Diamond Jubilee.

THE FRIENDS' MEETING HOUSE, a Grade II* listed building in Skinnergate, began on this site in 1678. In 1760 separate Meeting Houses for men and women were provided and the cottages in front used as almshouses. In 1839

the present front probably designed by **Joshua Sparkes** replaced the cottages. At the rear is the private burial ground where most of the influential Quaker families who dominated local government and industry last century are buried, with simple matching headstones.

THE MECHANICS' INSTITUTE, 1853, has a stately classical facade. It was designed by **Joshua Sparkes**, to whose business Richardson and Ross succeeded in 1855. A year after their partnership was dissolved, **J.P. Pritchett** enlarged the institute in 1863. Its hall would seat over five hundred. Here were small meeting rooms and a library. Winter classes in art and science were held. More recently the Institute housed a billiard room, a cinema and a bank. It is now a bar-diner.

Darlington's busy and popular Skinnergate

SKINNERGATE used to hold the sheep market, and still preserves something of a country air in its slightly curving line and its cottage-like properties with pantiled roofs. Some were still thatched into the later C18th. Much hand-made brick is in evidence as, for example, around the entrance arch to Clark's Yard. **Clark's, Buckton's and Mechanics' Yards** house small businesses whose setting is being enhanced. Blue scoriaceous double brick tiles have been an attractive flooring material characteristic of many of the town's hundred or so yards. The more recent **Court Arcade** with its upper facade dated 1912 was a cinema.

BONDGATE'S WIDE CENTRE was the medieval green of the Bishop's bond tenants, and held the common forge and bakehouse near Skinnergate corner. A central row of pantiled cottages is shown in an old print, and some cottages were still thatched in old Edward Pease's lifetime. In 1862 the central market area for Irish lean cattle was railed in, the footpaths paved and a drinking fountain put up by the town's **Temperance Society** in memory of its founder **Dr John Fothergill**. There were about twenty yards, housing craftsmen and merchants. A few were inhabited as late as the 1960s. **Mass Yard** held an early place of worship for the Roman Catholic community.

PRESENT DAY BONDGATE has several properties of interest: **No 5-6**, an Art Nouveau cafe, now a building society; **No. 22-23 The Turk's Head** late C17th/C18th; **No. 81** a classical stone building with Greek columns; **The Britannia Inn**, modest birthplace of the publisher **J.M. Dent**; **The Midland Bank** in white stone, an effective 'stopper' to the view along High Row.

CROWN STREET, made in the mid-C19th, holds a number of properties designed by **George Gordon Hoskins**: Crown Street Chambers (1886) as offices for a Quaker stockbroker William Harding; Nos. 3-7 Todd Bros, drapery and soft furnishings emporium (1902), now divided into four, with brown glazed tiling; the former North Star newspaper offices and printing works on Quebec Street corner (1882-9) with Dutch gables and tall reeded chimneys. Down East Street were the Darlington Poor Law Union Offices (1896), later the Registry Office now demolished.

THE EDWARD PEASE FREE LIBRARY (1884) by **Hoskins**, an exuberant Renaissance creation in red brick and red sandstone, was extended in similar style in 1933. The Library was built with a legacy of Edward Pease, a grandson of 'the father of railways'. A marble bust of the donor is in the original corner entrance hall. Behind the library were the chimney and weaving sheds of Pease's Woollen Mill, and across Lower Priestgate the offices, spinning mill and a corn mill, after which the **Cornmill Centre** on either side of Priestgate is named. This prestigious new shopping centre (1990-1992) is tucked behind the adjacent blocks, with entrances from Northgate, Prebends Row and Tubwell Row.

THE KING'S HEAD (1890) by **Hoskins**, replaced a coaching inn of 1661. A 'stopper' for the view down Bondgate, its main entrance was designed to be on Northgate, with shops as an original feature. Its elaborate Renaissance styling in red brick and red sandstone echoes that of buildings on Crown Street. Inside, were a grand staircase of American walnut and a banqueting hall and ballroom. An archway led to extensive stabling and coach houses at the rear.

THE STATUE OF JOSEPH PEASE by **G.A. Lawson** was unveiled in 1875 on 27th September, the Golden Jubilee Day of the opening of the Stockton and Darlington Railway. The main concerns of this first ever Quaker MP are shown on four bronze panels: Parliament, Schools, Railways and Anti-slavery. The statue was moved from its first island site nearby.

The new Cornmill Shopping Centre (CM)

HIGH ROW dominates the town centre from above its row of Shap granite steps formerly surmounted by iron railings supported between dark granite pillars with vases. These replaced a slope where the fat cattle market was held. Building facades ranging from the early C18th to the period between the wars harmonise with occasional later refrontings. Note a rainwater head dated 1733 and some unusual upper window arrangements. Rear premises may be older. Until the early C19th, traders lived above their shops. North of the gap formed by Post House Wynd are several substantial bank buildings. At the south end of High Row, Binns department store, begun by a firm of northern origin, culminates the view from the market square.

BACKHOUSES BANK, High Row, merged with Barclays in 1896. In ashlar sandstone with granite pillars, dormers, steep roofs and soaring chimneys, this Gothic building (1864) designed by **Alfred Waterhouse** was likened to an Italian Palace. A Grade II* listed building, it was restored in 1974 to celebrate the bicentenary of the founding of the Quaker family bank by **James Backhouse of West Lodge**, Darlington. Until the merger, all seventeen directors were Backhouses.

Myths, Legends & Folklore

Tradition holds that churches dedicated to St Cuthbert mark places where the Saxon monks paused in their wanderings with his intact body after leaving Lindisfarne in 875 AD and settling at Chester-le-Street in 883 and Durham in 995.

LADY JARRATT, daughter of **Bishop Cosin**, haunted the Bishop's Palace and hid in an underground passage to St Cuthbert's Church. Murdered by soldiers who cut off her arm to acquire a ring, she wandered at midnight and sunrise, rattling pans and removing bedclothes, especially before births and deaths in the workhouse which succeeded the Palace. Her silk dress rustled. She frightened children crossing the Skerne and ran about the market place disguised as a white rabbit. Also in the Palace was an oak chest, said to be enchanted, which nobody dared open.

A HOUSE IN TUBWELL ROW was troubled by someone continually grinding coffee, who could, however, be hushed by slightly opening a door. A boy was scared by a phantom white calf with large eyes, which proved to be a dog. Meanwhile, the ghostly white rabbit which nightly haunted Tubwell Row and market place turned out to be a real one!

A HIGH ROW LEGEND that a strong wind once blew out a dog's tongue arose when the corroded metal tongue of the talbot fell off the sign of the Talbot Inn on the corner of Post House Wynd. The ghost of **Joseph Pease** is said to haunt the site where his statue was first erected, an island in the road junction at the end of High Row.

BULMER'S STONE, on Northgate, a large Shap granite boulder formerly on the pavement but now behind the old technical college railings, was said to be where linen workers beat their flax and also where a town crier, **Billy Bulmer**, mounted to read out the news. Legends also surround old Edward Pease's house opposite, one being that **George Stephenson and his companion** having walked from Killingworth removed their boots before calling, or alternatively put their boots on, having come barefoot.

BEAUMONT HILL farther north, is supposed to be named after the capture there by brigands in 1317 of **Louis Beaumont**, bishop designate of Durham.

A WALK BY THE RIVER SKERNE between Ketton Bridge and Barmpton is wryly known as the **Welsh Mountains**, perhaps the nearest reminder of home to the Welsh ironworkers of the Rise Carr District. Flint arrow heads found at Newton Ketton and allegedly made by fairies were known as fairy stones, and could cure illnesses and ward off evil spirits. **Rock Well**, by the river at Haughton-le-Skerne, was also frequented by fairies, whilst travellers on the Haughton road near **Throstle Nest** were beset by strange forms resembling maidens and cats. On Parkgate, the ghost of **Signor Pepi**, first manager of the Hippodrome, haunts the stalls at Civic Theatre rehearsals, while his dog, buried in the theatre, whines around the main staircase.

BESIDE THE TEES, **Hob Headless** haunted the road between Hurworth and Neasham, but could not cross the Kent Beck. **Peg Fowler** with her green hair was a goblin of the Tees who would grab children who came too near the water. **Hell Kettles** are ponds near the Tees near Croft, which exploded into existence at Christmas 1179. Legends abound of their origin by earthquake, as bottomless pits of green water, an enormous pike, ducks, a goose and a cow which swam underground to the Tees, and a farmer with horse and haycart swallowed without trace. The old Baydale Beck Inn by the Borough boundary was the meeting place of **Catton's Gang**, so feared that it was avoided after dark. It was also haunted by **Sir William Browne**, executed for returning from transportation. **Dick Turpin** was reputed to frequent it. Rebuilt, the inn became fashionable for its oatcakes and whiskey. The Baydale Beck itself now takes extra water from the Cocker Beck, where the legendary joke of **Cockerton Docks** dies hard. It arose from a proposed C18th canal with a wharf at Cockerton.

BLACKWELL is well supplied with hauntings. At **Blackwell Grange** was the panelled room where the dead customarily lay in state. In the village, the deserted manor house of the Prescotts, who owned Blackwell before the Allans came, was haunted by **Old Pinkney** in his red nightcap. In Blackwell Lane were found the bones of **Cecily Kirby**, a servant girl murdered there by **Sam Addy**, a soldier heading for Culloden, where she appeared to him as he lay dying on the battlefield. At **Glassensykes**, a beck by Harewood Grove, wraith-like dogs, cats, rabbits, goblins and headless men and women appeared, no doubt transmutations of mists along the Skerne.

Entertainment in the Past

In olden times, the ducking stool and the bull ring, bear baiting, ox roasting and elections provided public entertainment, as did the passage of important people through the town or to the Bishop's Palace.

The interesting style of Darlington Civic Theatre (CT)

IN VICTORIAN TIMES, newly elected MPs were hauled through the town in their carriages by a willing mass of human hands. Local election results were announced to crowds gathered below the steps of the covered market. Long funeral processions of important townsfolk were marked by the closure of shops, the tolling of bells and the gathering of crowds of spectators en route. When **Queen Victoria, Prince Albert and the royal children** paused at Bank Top Station in 1849, the station had been repainted and decorated, church bells pealed, shops closed, thousands assembled along the lines, a loyal address was presented, there was a bonfire and fireworks and the day was a public holiday. **The Golden Jubilee of the Stockton and Darlington Railway** was also a great occasion, and a **Railway Carnival** became an annual event, recently revived. The Central Hall in Bull Wynd was the venue for balls, public meetings and entertainments. **Franz Liszt** played in town, and **Charles Dickens** gave a reading in the old town hall in 1862. Educational events went on in reading rooms and at meetings, especially under Quaker influence. The Mechanics Institute, the Temperance Hall and Cocoa Palaces provided sober activities and refreshment.

THEATRES GAINED A FOOTHOLD, if somewhat transient, despite Quaker misgivings. A travelling tent theatre is recorded on Whit Monday 1772. In the early C19th **Thorn's Theatre** came to Clay Row and later to Blackwellgate. Assembly rooms were used as theatres behind the Sun Inn on High Row and the Golden Cock in Tubwell Row. In 1858 the **Barn Theatre** opened in a wooden building behind the Green Tree Inn, Skinnergate. The first **Theatre Royal**, with wooden benches, built in Buck's Close in 1865 failed. A new Theatre Royal in 1881 in Northgate soon burnt down, The third Theatre Royal in 1887, with facilities as we expect them, lasted with plays, music hall, varieties and films until 1936, when a cinema was built on its site. The **Central Hall** was also converted to a cinema, as was part of the Mechanics' Institute.

The popular Arts Centre in Darlington

The **Hippodrome**, however, built in Parkgate in 1907, survived, and as the **Civic Theatre** has been restored to its Edwardian comfort as one of the most successful theatres in the country. Its first manager, **Signor Rino Pepi** died in 1927 on the very day that **Pavlova** performed there. Before the First World War artistes included George Robey, Harry Lauder, Florrie Ford, Wee Georgie Wood, Evelyn Laye, the Carl Rosa Company and the D'Oyly Carte Opera Company. The 1930s and 1940s welcomed George Formby, Nellie Wallace and the Sadlers Wells Theatre Ballet. Recent years have seen Dame Margot Fonteyn, Dame Anna Neagle, Dorothy Tutin, Chris Bonnington, Cilla Black, Mike Yarwood, Ken Dodd, Peter Sallis, Cleo Lane and John Dankworth, Scottish Opera and The Northern Sinfonia, to name but a few famous performers at what is now Darlington Civic Theatre.

Green Spaces to Enjoy

All parts of Darlington are within reasonable walking distance of open countryside. Villages with pleasant greens dot the rural areas around the town, and there are riverside walks along the Tees and the Skerne. The Borough has a long tradition of enlightened enhancement. Newer housing estates include open grassed areas often with preserved mature trees, and grass verges are frequent. Roundabouts have seasonally changed floral displays, and planted vases and hanging baskets are a summer feature in the town centre. There are no less than nineteen parks, open spaces and recreation grounds.

SOUTH PARK is by far the largest, about 40 hectares (100 acres). It began as **Poor Howdens Farm**, 8 hectares (20 acres) gifted to the town in 1636 by James Bellasis as a charitable trust, and became in 1853 **Bellasis Park**, one of the earliest public parks in the North. It was laid out along a tree-lined promenade, with an entrance in Grange Road. In 1880, lower land nearer the town was developed as a sports and show ground, lake, bandstand and shrubberies with direct access from town via Victoria Embankment. In 1924, **Geneva Bridge and Road** (later renamed Parkside) were built, more land was brought in along Grange Road and a new main entrance made from the south. When **Blackwell Meadows** came into the Borough in 1930, the Park was extended beyond Parkside, and a lagoon along the Skerne in the old park widened out into an extensive boating lake beside the old Blackwell corn mill. After the lake silted, this area was landscaped as a pitch and putt course.

South Park trees are a delight: willows by the water, a lime avenue by the Skerne, weeping ash, soaring Wellingtonia and a variety of broadleaves and conifers. In the early days Mayors were encouraged to plant for their year of office. Joseph Pease donated exotic specimens. Trees were planted to mark special occasions. These include two now massive sequoias in 1863 for the wedding of Edward Prince of Wales with Alexandra, oaks for the coronations in 1902 and 1911 of Edward VII and George V and a Japanese cherry in commemoration of all Far Eastern victims of the Second World War. A **tropical garden** was later made around Henry Pease's Pierremont fountain. In 1952 the **Chandler Rose Garden** was planted with eight hundred rose bushes. Recently a **buddleia border** was introduced to attract butterflies. Floral designs are created each year near to the clock tower.

The lake has resident flocks of geese, ducks and swans, coots and moorhens. Other amenities include a **bandstand** of 1893, a **rustic tea-room** 1908, three **aviaries**, the **bowling greens** of 1901 (the first in Darlington) and 1932, **tennis courts, putting green**, a **model boat pool**, and a **roller skating rink** of 1938, a contribution to the Keep Fit Movement, then in vogue. **Official memorabilia** include rails and stone sleepers from the S&DR 1825; a Russian cannon from the Crimean War 1853-56; the memorial to John Fowler, inventor of the multiple steam plough, 1856; a memorial from Bondgate, 1862, to John Fothergill, Chairman of the Darlington Total Abstinence Society; a glacial erratic boulder of Shap granite in recognition of geologist R. Taylor Manson, 1900; and the clock tower, 1901, memorial to William Potts, manufacturer of public clocks.

South Park's tremendous colours and character

BRINKBURN DENE is a linear park along the Cocker Beck between Cockerton and Northgate. It includes the entrance on Woodland Road to **Brinkburn**, the former mansion of Henry Fell Pease and has tennis courts, play areas and spring daffodils.

THE CROCUS WALK along Grange Road and Southend Avenue was formerly **The Rookery**, the shelter belt behind the park wall of Joseph

Pease's mansion Southend. This woodland was saved by Darlington Borough Council in 1901 when the parkland was built over. Beech, oak, horse-chestnut and sycamore predominate, with turkey oak, red oak, a Spanish chestnut, a few limes, a Lawson cypress and a Wellingtonia adding variety. Yew and holly make a dark foil to thousands of snowdrops and crocuses. **Green Park**, off Coniscliffe Road, was also part of Joseph's Southend parkland.

Beauty and serenity at Darlington's Stanhope Park

STANHOPE PARK gave a pleasant setting for the **Grammar School of Queen Elizabeth** (now the Sixth Form College) and **Darlington Training College** (now the Arts Centre) in Vane Terrace. It was planted in the 1870s when the Duke of Cleveland's estate was being built over.

NORTH LODGE PARK, Northgate, became a public park in 1901, the remnant of a larger private park around William Backhouse's villa **Elmfield**. This had already been subdivided to allow grounds for John Beaumont Pease's villa **North Lodge**, from which land for the **Technical College** was later taken. A fish pond with a castellated boathouse was kept, to be fed by surplus water from Gladstone Street swimming baths. Skating was popular in winter. In 1903 came a bandstand and in 1906 the bowling green pavilion. A bandstand open air school was held for a while. When Elmfield was sold in 1920 its ground came into the park, but in 1932 the lake was filled in, and in 1954 the boathouse demolished.

THE HERITAGE GARDEN in **Bull Wynd** was once the walled garden of Edward Pease's house, hemmed in by outbuildings in Chancery Lane until landscaped. The ornate cast iron fountain is part of a larger one erected in Tubwell Row in 1858. From its later position in Green Park it was moved in 1970 to mark the centenary of the first publication in Darlington of the Northern Echo.

THE TOWN HALL AND GROUNDS occupy the site of the Bishop's Palace, almshouses, Leadyard and Feethams, the home of Joseph Pease Senior. Lawns and young trees spread down to the landscaped banks of the Skerne overhung with willows.

ST CUTHBERT'S CHURCHYARD is another green haven in the town centre, opened out in 1971. Mature trees were retained, new ones planted, lawns laid, attractive gravestones preserved, daffodils planted and seats provided. Now the Church's ancient beauty can be appreciated.

WEST CEMETERY, Carmel Road, was made in 1857, St Cuthbert's churchyard having been closed for burials. The land was part of **Salutation Farm**. Mortuary chapels are in Early English Gothic. The cemetery paths form quiet walks amongst an amazing variety of trees, especially conifers, many of them unusual, in what has become virtually a nature reserve and arboretum as well as a repository of the town's history. Here, non-Quakers who played a part in the town's Victorian and subsequent prosperity are remembered, including **Francis Mewburn** the last Bishop's bailiff and first railway solicitor, **G.G. Hoskins** prolific architect, **R.H. Allan of Blackwell** and a host of ordinary townsfolk.

CEMETERY LANE AND NUNNERY LANE between Carmel Road and Edinburgh Drive form pleasant walks through mature woodland, the former shelter belts for Arthur Pease's park at Hummersknott.

THE RIVER TEES provides a favourite riverbank walk through open countryside between **Broken Scar Picnic Area** and **Blackwell Village**. A **Nature Trail** leaflet and fishing permits are available from Darlington Borough Council. Riverside paths can also be followed from **Low** to **High Coniscliffe**, and from **Middleton-One-Row** to **Low Dinsdale**.

THE RIVER SKERNE, recently landscaped, can be followed from **Haughton-le-Skerne Bridge** across **Rockwell Pasture** and beside a nature reserve to **Albert Road**. The Skerne can also be followed from **Barmpton Bridge** to **Ketton Bridge** where several paths diverge.

Places to Visit in the Borough

Darlington is at the centre of a wide area of rolling countryside and high quality farmland dotted with pleasant villages, many around attractive greens.

CROFT on the Tees has an ancient stone bridge with seven ribbed arches, where each **Bishop of Durham**, on first entering his diocese, was presented with the falchion with which **Sir John Conyers** slew the legendary **Sockburn Worm**. **Croft Spa** was established in 1669 and the new Spa with a pump room and hot and cold baths in 1829. **Sir William Chaytor** built the Croft Spa Hotel in 1808. Apartment houses on both sides of the Tees catered for visitors, especially after the railway came. **The Rectory** was Lewis Carroll's home whilst his father, the Rev. Charles Dodgson, buried here, was rector (1843-1868). **St Peter's Church**, part Norman, has the amazing C17th **Milbanke family box pew** mounted on pillars. Lord Byron and Annabella Milbanke honeymooned at nearby Halnaby Hall in 1815.

HURWORTH is a residential village with a long, tapering green, pleasant houses and elegant villas. **The Old Hall, Hurworth House** and **Manor House** are early C18th, and the old **Rectory** early C19th. The mathematician **William Emerson** (1701-1782) lived here. The east end was formerly thronged with linen hand-loom weavers. **All Saints Church** was rebuilt in 1830. **Newbus Grange**, 1610 with Regency updating, is now a hotel.

NEASHAM had a medieval nunnery. **Abbey House, Neasham Hill House** and **Neasham Hall** in landscaped grounds and four market garden orchards made attractive a village formerly subject to Tees floods. A protective embankment now allows a riverside walk, and Neasham Hill grounds are open to the public.

MIDDLETON-ONE-ROW curves high above the Tees beside a steeply sloping green laced with paths made for visitors to the nearby spa. The village and hotel were rebuilt in the 1820s. As the spa declined, the village became residential, expanding westwards where a new **Church of St Lawrence** was built in 1871. To the east, **Low Middleton Hall**, refronted in 1721, caters for the creative use of leisure.

DINSDALE is a village in which a riverside path from Middleton-One-Row leads to **Dinsdale Spa**, discovered in 1789 whilst boring for coal. Early baths by the river were rebuilt in 1824, and a new seventy bedroom hydropathic hotel was built on the cliff above. In 1880 the baths were rebuilt as a small hotel, but the spa did not survive. The riverside woodland path leads on to **Dinsdale Church** built in 1196, the old rectory, and **Dinsdale Manor House**, the moated home of the Surtees family from the C12th.

LOW CONISCLIFFE a residential village by an old Tees ford, has the mounds of the medieval manor house of the **Greystoke** family. A riverside path leads to **High Coniscliffe**, or a well marked short cut returns via fields to the village.

HIGH CONISCLIFFE is also a starting point for a stroll by the Tees, below the dramatically sited rectory and Early English church on the 'king's cliff'. **St Edwin's** is uniquely dedicated to the Saxon King of Northumbria, slain in 633 AD, and contains fragments of Saxon cross shafts.

PIERCEBRIDGE is a village whose pretty whitewashed cottages face a rectangular green, built inside a Roman fort where **Dere Street** crossed the Tees. Excavated remains of the fort and Roman bridge are open to the public. Across the river, the **George Inn** has a grandfather clock which stopped when the licensee Jenkins died, supposedly the origin of the well-known song.

WALWORTH CASTLE was rebuilt in the C16th by **Thomas Jennison**, Auditor-General to Queen Elizabeth I. In 1603, his widow lavishly entertained the Scottish King on his way south to claim the English throne as James I. It is now a hotel with panoramic views.

REDWORTH HALL was the C17th home of the **Surtees** family who enlarged it in the C18th and again twice in the C19th. It is now a hotel and conference centre, towering steeply above the secluded village of Redworth.

Further Afield

For all information about the many attractions in a wider area around Darlington, we refer you to **Discovery Publishing (UK) Ltd's Best of Britain guides**, including 'Teesdale and the High Pennines', 'The City and County of Durham' and 'The Yorkshire Dales', as well as several smaller **Heritage guides** to individual Yorkshire Dales and two County Durham towns, **Barnard Castle and Middleton-in-Teesdale**.

The Cornmill Centre

The long-awaited Cornmill Shopping Centre opened on August 27, 1992. The Centre certainly has revolutionised shopping in Darlington; it has provided fifty new shops in an attractive modern environment, which compliments existing shops, the markets and leisure facilities in the town.

The Cornmill is built in an attractive architectural design, winner of the Mayor's Design Award, which sits comfortably amongst its historical neighbours in the heart of Darlington town centre.

A WHOLE NEW SHOPPING EXPERIENCE for all the family is waiting to be discovered inside at the Cornmill Centre, Darlington.

With close to fifty shops the Cornmill offers you complete shopping inside. The first choice for fashion, bringing you the latest styles for men, women and children, together with jewellery, shoes and fashion accessories. Music too, books, hi-fi and videos, toys, sportswear and stationery, in fact, everything you could wish to find under one roof.

Top quality speciality shops abound - not only the leading high street names like C&A and W H Smith, but shops selling everything from hats to spectacles, computers to household goods, fruit and vegetables to freshly baked patisserie.

Whether it's a cup of coffee whilst you pause for thought, fast food or a leisurely meal, you'll certainly be satisfied by the great value and great menus at the Cornmill's mall restaurants, Billy Bunter's Coffee House, Mark One Cafe and Burger King.

RELAX IN A CLEAN, SAFE, SHOPPING ENVIRONMENT, tastefully decorated with green plants and topped by a spectacular glass dome that fills the centre with light. Visit attractive craft barrows and enjoy a variety of mall entertainment and informative displays. Whether it's cold and rainy, or hot and sticky, the climate is always perfect for shopping in the Cornmill Centre.

Come to the Cornmill Centre, Darlington, with so much to see and do this is one shopping trip you'll never forget.

The Dolphin Centre

NUMBER ONE FOR BUSINESS OR LEISURE is how the Dolphin Centre is renowned as the North East's number one leisure, entertainment, conference and exhibition venue.

But don't just take our word for it. Ask any of the million plus visitors who enjoy its fabulous four pool water complex, excellent sports, fitness and health facilities and quality catering. The Dolphin Centre offers so much more. It hosts pop concerts, classical recitals, fashion shows, professional boxing and wrestling and exhibitions. The Centre's outstanding facilities and the sheer professionalism of its staff, make any event really special.

Exhibition organisers can choose from nine possible venue areas, ranging from rooms 50 square metres up to halls of 1200 square metres complete with electrical, lighting, audio-visual and public address systems. These facilities are also perfect for meetings, seminars and conferences, from small groups up to 1000 delegates.

Ancillary rooms are perfect for VIP guests, and press conferences, with an exhibition organiser control room available. The Dolphin Centre can even provide for a 400 person conference and 1200 square metres exhibition simultaneously.

The Dolphin Centre has an enviable reputation for producing excellent catering and its comprehensive facilities include a fully licensed lounge bar, restaurant and a self-service cafeteria.

So, whatever your requirements, whether business or leisure, make the Dolphin Centre your number one choice.

CATERING FOR ALL TASTES, the Dolphin Centre has excellent catering facilities available in all halls, with the Restaurant and Meeting Rooms perfect for larger parties, and the Committee Room or Pepperpot suitable for numbers up to 25.

The Waterfront Bar is open during normal licensed hours for a relaxing drink or bar meal, and the Self-Service Cafeteria offers a wide menu choice, including daily specials and vegetarian dishes.